AMERICAN WATER SPANIEL

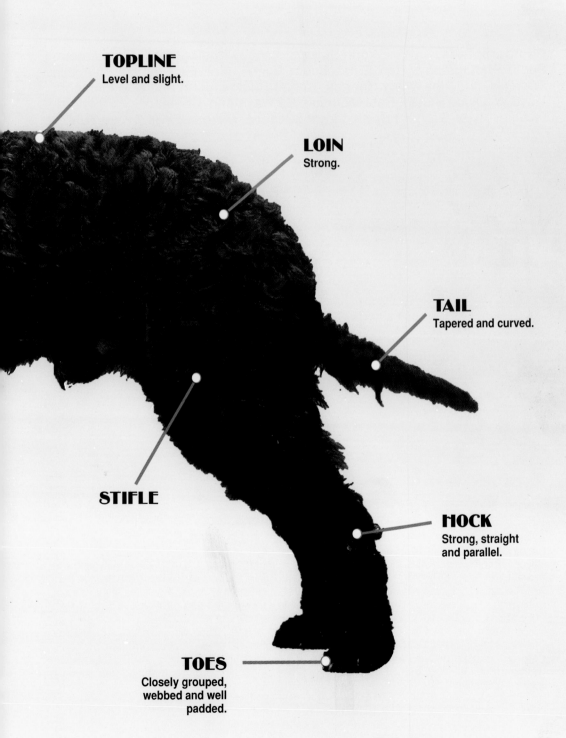

TOPLINE
Level and slight.

LOIN
Strong.

TAIL
Tapered and curved.

STIFLE

HOCK
Strong, straight
and parallel.

TOES
Closely grouped,
webbed and well
padded.

Title page: A trio of American Water Spaniels owned by Lara Suesens.

Photographers: Animal World Studios, Ashbey Photography, Mary Bloom, Booth Photography, Ron Ernst, Laura Evans, Gail Fitzsimmons, Isabelle Francais, Judy Iby, Mary Kangas, Kohler Photos, John and Sue Liemohn, Lloyd W. Olson Studio, Paul Morrison, Bill Raymond, Constance Rutherford, Heather Rygs, Barbara Spisak, Lara Suesens, Margaret Will, Missy Yuhl.

© by T.F.H. Publications, Inc.

Distributed in the UNITED STATES to the Pet Trade by T.F.H. Publications, Inc., One T.F.H. Plaza, Neptune City, NJ 07753; distributed in the UNITED STATES to the Bookstore and Library Trade by National Book Network, Inc. 4720 Boston Way, Lanham MD 20706; in CANADA to the Pet Trade by H & L Pet Supplies Inc., 27 Kingston Crescent, Kitchener, Ontario N2B 2T6; Rolf C. Hagen Inc., 3225 Sartelon St. Laurent-Montreal Quebec H4R 1E8; in CANADA to the Book Trade by Vanwell Publishing Ltd., 1 Northrup Crescent, St. Catharines, Ontario L2M 6P5 ; in ENGLAND by T.F.H. Publications, PO Box 15, Waterlooville PO7 6BQ; in AUSTRALIA AND THE SOUTH PACIFIC by T.F.H. (Australia), Pty. Ltd., Box 149, Brookvale 2100 N.S.W., Australia; in NEW ZEALAND by Brooklands Aquarium Ltd. 5 McGiven Drive, New Plymouth, RD1 New Zealand; in Japan by T.F.H. Publications, Japan—Jiro Tsuda, 10-12-3 Ohjidai, Sakura, Chiba 285, Japan; in SOUTH AFRICA by Lopis (Pty) Ltd., P.O. Box 39127, Booysens, 2016, Johannesburg, South Africa. Published by T.F.H. Publications, Inc.

MANUFACTURED IN THE
UNITED STATES OF AMERICA
BY T.F.H. PUBLICATIONS, INC.

AMERICAN WATER SPANIEL

A COMPLETE AND RELIABLE HANDBOOK

Constance Rutherford

RX-109

CONTENTS

HISTORY OF THE AMERICAN WATER SPANIEL

The American Water Spaniel was developed in the Midwest as a multi-purpose hunter. He was used by the old-time meat hunters of the 1800s, and his field of activity encompassed a wide variety of game. Ducks, geese, grouse, pheasant, quail, woodcock, rabbit, and squirrel were displaced and retrieved with dispatch. His curly coat repelled the thorny brush and was insulating and waterproof, leaving him indifferent to the frigid temperatures. His tough footpads suited him well for long consecutive days of hunting.

The American Water Spaniel was developed as a multi-purpose hunter in the Midwest during the 1800s. Owner, Lara Suesens.

But what the old timers said of him in comparison to other sporting breeds was that he had "moxie"—the ability to face difficulty with spirit. Into the thicket he would go in search of cripples, admirably persistent in his efforts. Being several inches shorter than the setters, pointers, and retrievers, he could slip beneath the branches of the bramble, nose to ground, tail whipping eagerly as he neared his quarry.

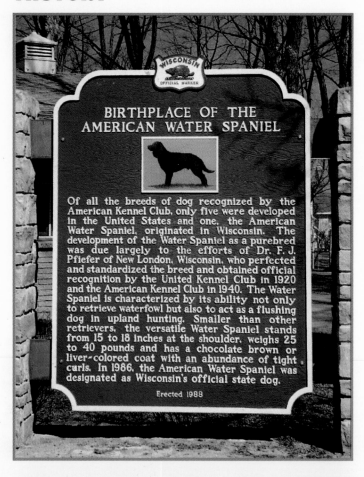

This sign commemorates the birthplace of the American Water Spaniel in New London, Wisconsin. Photo courtesy of Lara Suesens.

This hunting savvy and spirit of moxie, combined in a dog of medium size, had been developed by American sportsmen at a time when meat was hunted for the table, the hunting parties traveling miles of river in canoe or skiff. Frequently they stayed in the marsh, sleeping in the skiff to await the sunrise shooting. The large retrievers, while powerful and capable, had been found to be a hazard in the canoe. So, the versatile, compact American Water Spaniel with its curled, protective coat became a common sight in Midwest marsh and field.

The American Water Spaniel has been a familiar sight in the area of Oshkosh, Wisconsin since 1850, valued as a hunting dog. No records of its development exist. There is a close similarity to the English Water Spaniel, now extinct. This English hunter was of like size and credited with exceptional scenting powers. Most were of brown coloring, though black specimens were found. To enhance its soft, fine coat, unsuitable for Midwest waterfowl hunting, it is be-

An excellent example of an early American Water Spaniel, Caramel Candy, CDX bred by Americana Kennels won Best of Breed in 1963 and 1964.

lieved that crosses were made to the Curly-Coated Retriever. A further contribution may have come from the small Irish Water Spaniel, said to have existed in the St. John's region of Newfoundland. Though we can only speculate, these crossbred dogs were culled and linebred, genetically setting the traits and stature of what was then referred to as the American Brown Water Spaniel.

Dr. Fred J. Pfeiffer of New London, Wisconsin is credited with a prominent portion of this breed's

The American Water Spaniel has a long history of hunting and water retrieval. Ch. Americana's Little Beaver, CD during a training session in 1965.

history. In the early 1900s, as a young boy, he had come to hunt with and value the breed, which was very common near New London, Wisconsin. Later in his life it was he who sustained the breed during the drought of the 1930s and Depression years that followed. In 1938 a breed club was formed of a handful of breeders; they developed the breed standard, and recognition by the UKC followed in 1939.

Opposite: Americana Wahoo, CDX owned by C.A. Frank won his CD degree in three straight shows. He was also the applause-inducing clown in Charlie's Dog Retrieving Act seen by thousands throughout the Midwest in the 1960s.

Chief Navigator, an American Water Spaniel from the 1950s, launching into a retrieve from a 6-foot diving board.

The American Kennel Club recognized the breed in 1940.

Most American Waters of today are equal to their counterparts of long ago. They are still loved and valued by their families as protectors and companions. During the hunting season they can put in long, hard days of hunting with admirable results. Tough-footed, with stamina, the spirit of moxie is still evident. Those who make them their companions find inherent perceptions and intelligence that give new meaning to the words. Our American Water has been and still is a multi-purpose hunter of the Midwest, and beloved companion to Americans with heart.

Sadly, it must be mentioned here, that the American Water Spaniel is classified neither as spaniel nor retriever, and is therefore not eligible to compete in AKC spaniel hunting tests or retriever trials.

Today's American Waters possess the instincts, confidence and intelligence of their early ancestors. Ch. Americana's Little Beaver CD owned by Tom Rutherford and bred by Americana Kennels.

DESCRIPTION OF THE AMERICAN WATER SPANIEL

The American Water Spaniel is an intelligent and spirited dog by nature, with a readiness to be a part of the action. Being larger than a Cocker Spaniel and smaller than an English Springer Spaniel, he is neither too large for travel in the back seat of a car nor too

The ultimate companion and family dog, the American Water Spaniel thrives on the attention he receives from his owners. Jane Christiansen with an American Water puppy.

small to put in a good day of hunting as a flushing spaniel and retriever. His coat of liver or chocolate brown consists of curled or wavy hair of medium length and is protective in the coldest weather.

As a companion, he is at his very best. In the family as a watchdog, he barks to announce the approaching stranger, then accepts him after the family has

13

The versatility of the American Water Spaniel allows him to excel at many tasks, including the job of therapy dog. This guy has brought some joy to the life of this Alzhiemer's patient.

extended a welcome. Some of advanced age are said to exhibit a discernment of strangers, revealing an uncanny perception of human character and intent.

Within the family unit he is patient with, protective of, and loyal to the children, though he expects to be treated with respect. In the winter, he will run beside the children's sleds as they race down snow-covered hills. In the summer he's a fishing companion, watching the floating bobber with anticipation. In the fall, he fires with enthusiasm at the sight of the shotgun, ready to put in arduous days in the field or marsh. And at the end of the day, as weary as the little children, you'll find him curled contentedly within the family circle—he's their protector.

The versatile American Water Spaniel can be found among groups of therapy dogs that serve in health care facilities, or participating in agility and flyball competitions—performing as the showman that we suspect he has always been. The intelligent, stable disposition has always been the primary asset of this breed; the essential element of family pet, companion, obedience dog, bench champion, and hunter.

TEMPERAMENT

Typically, the American Water Spaniel possesses a "spaniel-like" temperament—happy, eager, ready to participate. This temperament is the result of the genetic mix that has been passed down to him by his ancestors. However, a dog's disposition is not all genetically inherited. Much of what a dog displays in his individual personality is the result of his experiences through the various stages of his life.

From nutrition to hygiene to just plain old love, the mother of a litter will provide the puppies with everything they need. Noma's Upland Empress owned by Mary Kangas with her litter.

In his early environment, was his confidence increased by being taken from the litter for individual attention by the breeder (and children), instilling in him a sense that the world is good? (This socialization is extremely important to the development of confidence and trust). Or, was he one of a litter that was raised like barn-dwelling livestock in seclusion, with little human attention? In this atmosphere, the mother of the litter is the leader, the pup a member of her pack. What will she teach him of her own experiences—that man is the infrequent stranger and to regard him with distrust?

DESCRIPTION

The next phase of a dog's young life is also influential, as he still remains impressionable in his developing attitude after being taken from his mother and siblings. Was he brought into a family unit, raised as a responsible member of it, and taught good citizenship? Or, was he placed by himself in a kennel, in solitary confinement, and given little human attention or training?

As you can see, it is the investment of ourselves, our time and patient caring, that is required for the development of a companion dog. Through this interaction, intelligence is increased, willingness to please is captured, and intuition is enhanced. It can be concluded that most problem dogs are the result of "human errors" in dog handling.

When a dog or puppy arrives in his new home, it will take time for him to acclimate and to accept his boundaries and routine of the household. He should be treated with respect by the children and not overwhelmed by their attentions when he is really little more than a stranger. Devotion will develop over time. Perhaps it is a strong "pack instinct" that allows the breed such reserve. He tends to be a one-family dog, and often attaches himself with a strong bond to one member of the family.

Make sure your new puppy is well supervised and knows his boundaries in his new home. This little fellow looks like he could get into a lot of trouble if you let him! Owner, Lara Suesens.

American Water Spaniels have a natural propensity for water that makes them inherent retrievers. This puppy is getting his "feet wet" for the first time. Owner, Lara Suesens.

There are those of us who have known and loved this marvelous breed throughout our lives. We respect and intend to preserve all of its wonderful attributes: structure, coat, soundness, intelligence, disposition, and hunting prowess. To do this, it must be the prevailing mission of *all* breeders to effect stability in our breed. Only through a broad purpose can we ensure that each successive generation remains true to its heritage. Surely, our many-faceted American Water Spaniel deserves a continuing place in the American home.

NATURAL INSTINCT

What if a young child was born with the ability to drive a car? His parents had for generations been able to do so, and therefore, he was passed that ability upon reaching a particular age. This is an example of innate ability. The following is an example of inherited retrieving ability as witnessed by the author.

The river before us was nearly 30 feet across. Standing beside it, we could see dark, silent streaks of current far into the middle, indicating that it was deep. Tom, raising a large broken piece of tree limb over his head, tossed it with effort to a distance of nearly 12 feet. Beside me I heard, "Jody, fetch," in a strong, commanding voice.

Our dog was young, just over a year old, and had been a kennel dog to the age of eight months when we

17

bought him. No field experience had he been given. Little did he know of retrieving and water current.

We watched him intently, then glanced toward the large, bobbing limb that had been thrown for him to retrieve. It twisted slightly as the current swept it along, bringing to it a quality of aliveness. With a whine, Jody stepped into the water and for a fleeting moment it appeared through eagerness that he would leap from the bank where he stood. If he had, he would never have been able to intercept the tree limb, for it was moving too fast. Instead, he turned and began running downstream, skirting the bushes along the shore. About 75 feet downstream he stopped, measured his distance to the limb, and then leaped into the rushing current. To our amazement it was not

Field training begins at an early age. This six-week-old pup is being introduced to bird scent by carrying and playing with a bird wing. Owner, Paul Morrison.

toward the branch that he swam but directly to the center of the stream. With his head held high in order to see his moving target, he adjusted slightly, like an outfielder aligning himself beneath a fly ball. When he reached the middle of the stream, the limb approached him, he grasped it firmly, turned, and maneuvered it across the current to us.

Today, many years from this event, we can marvel at the genetic precision that enabled this remarkable feat. With no first-hand experience or handling, this dog, who had been raised in kennel isolation, had been passed the genetic mix that would enable this superb retrieve. These abilities were certainly inherited, a legacy of his ancestors, and they could not have done it better.

STANDARD FOR THE AMERICAN WATER SPANIEL

A standard is a written description of the "ideal dog," a dog that in actuality has never existed and never will. The following standard is the approved standard of the American Kennel Club, the principal governing body for the dog sport in the United States. The standard is drafted and proposed by the national parent club, and then accepted by the AKC. As the parent club sees fit, the standard can change from time to time, though these changes are essentially quite minor, usually pertaining to the format of the

A standard describes the ideal traits of a particular breed of dog. Ch. Waterway's Alley Oop owned by Pamela Boyer and Linda Hattrem.

The American Water Spaniel is an active, muscular dog of compact build. Ch. Just Plain Ol' Taylor shown by Linda Hattrem winning Best of Breed.

standard itself or perhaps some word choice. Studying the breed standard will reveal much about the dog itself, its character, and its ideal physique. Whether you are interested in breeding, showing, or just enjoying your dog, the standard makes required reading for any breed fancier.

General Appearance—The American Water Spaniel was developed in the United States as an all-around hunting dog, bred to retrieve from skiff or canoes and work ground with relative ease. The American Water Spaniel is an active muscular dog, medium in size with a marcel to curly coat. Emphasis is placed on proper size and a symmetrical relationship of parts, texture of coat and color.

Size, Proportion, Substance—15 to 18 inches for either sex. Males weighing 30–45 lbs. Females weighing 25–40 lbs. Females tend to be slightly smaller than the males. There is no preference for size within the given range of either sex providing correct proportion, good substance and balance is maintained. *Proportion* is slightly longer than tall, not too square or compact. However, exact proportion is not as important as the dog being well-balanced and sound, capable of performing the breed's intended function. **Substance**, a solidly built and well-muscled dog full of strength and quality. The breed has as much substance and bone as necessary to carry the muscular structure but not so much as to appear clumsy.

Head—The head must be in proportion to the overall dog. Moderate in length. **Expression** is alert, self-confident, attractive and intelligent. Medium size **eyes** set well apart, while slightly rounded, should not

Ch. Waterway's Be-Bop-A-Lulu, SD owned by Linda and John Hattrem.

appear protruding or bulging. Lids tight, not drooping. Eye color can range from a light yellowish brown to brown, hazel or of dark tone to harmonize with coat. Disqualify yellow eyes. Yellow eyes are a bright color like that of a lemon, not to be confused with the light yellowish brown. Ears set slightly above the eye line, but not too high on the head, lobular, long and wide with the leather extending to nose.

Skull rather broad and full, **stop** moderately defined, but not too pronounced. **Muzzle** moderate in length, square with good depth. No inclination to snipiness. The lips are clean and tight without excess skin or flews. Nose dark in color, black or dark brown. The nose sufficiently wide and with well-developed nostrils to insure good scenting power. **Bite** either scissor or level.

Neck, Topline, Body—Neck round and of medium length, strong and muscular, free of throatiness, set to carry head with dignity, but arch not accentuated. **Topline** level or slight, straight slope from withers. **Body** well-developed, sturdily constructed but not too compactly coupled. Well-developed brisket extending to elbow neither too broad nor too narrow. The ribs well-sprung, but not so well-sprung that they interfere with the movement of the front assembly. The loins strong, but not having a tucked-

The texture of the American Water Spaniel's protective outer coat can range from uniform waves to close curls. Owner, Lara Suesens.

up look. **Tail** is moderate in length, curved in a rocker fashion, can be carried either slightly below or above the level of the back. The tail is tapered, lively and covered with hair with moderate feathering.

Forequarters—Shoulders sloping, clean and muscular. Legs medium in length, straight and well-boned but not so short as to handicap for field work or so heavy as to appear clumsy. Pasterns strong with no suggestion of weakness. Toes closely grouped, webbed and well-padded. Size of feet to harmonize with size of dog. Front dewclaws are permissible.

key to unlocking his great potential. Your puppy, being young and impressionable, can become more aware, intelligent, discerning, and worldly through his experiences. You are urged to make a close companion of him by living with him, including him in your life, and allowing him to know you well. The American Water Spaniel is at his very best as a companion.

Conversely, as a kennel dog he does not excel. He will be resented by the neighbors for his barking; teased by local children when you are not at home, soon soured in disposition. When taken to the field to run after days of confinement, is it any wonder the "prisoner" applies his freedom of choice, leaving you behind? It is only with an investment of yourself, your

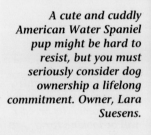

A cute and cuddly American Water Spaniel pup might be hard to resist, but you must seriously consider dog ownership a lifelong commitment. Owner, Lara Suesens.

time, your patience, and your interaction that you will produce an American Water Spaniel who is a companion of distinction.

MALE OR FEMALE?

Before the purchase of a puppy you should consider the eventual purpose for your dog—family pet, hunter, etc. Unless your dog develops into one of exceptional quality, she should not be bred. Although it is enticing to predict that a litter will pay for the purchase price of your female, this is seldom the case. Too often a purebred female escapes only to be serviced by the neighbor's male, leaving you with a mixed litter of puppies to sell (or give away). There are also unforeseen veterinary expenses: whelping com-

away in the evening he will be safe from electrocution by chewing on a lamp cord, or from the hazardous ingestion of a plastic or rubber item that only an autopsy can reveal. If you intend to show him, the crate will be used on the show bench to restrict the attentions of people who may startle or upset your dog. And the crate will be most appreciated on hunting trips when it's time to return home with your wet, muddy dog.

Being away from mother, brothers, and sisters is a sad experience for your puppy. He will be confused and frightened, and you can expect him to howl when he is left alone. His activities will range from a flurry of activity to sporadic napping. When he is awake,

Opposite: Experiencing a loving relationship with a responsible child will help your puppy become a well-socialized dog. This is Erin Blandford with an American Water Spaniel pup.

To keep him out of trouble, give your American Water Spaniel a Nylabone®. It will keep him occupied while keeping his gums and teeth healthy.

constant supervision will prevent destructive chewing. As you know, electrical cords are most life threatening, but the loss of your favorite pair of shoes can bring you a good-sized jolt, too. So, provide a chew toy for his teething months. If you catch him chewing on something forbidden, scold him, then offer him a Gumabone® as a substitute. He'll catch on quickly enough. When he is older, provide hard Nylabones® from the pet shop, as they will keep him occupied while helping to keep his teeth and gums clean.

If you choose not to use the dog crate, there are many good dog beds available for young puppies. Make sure you place the bed in a warm, draft-free area and furnish it with a soft blanket or pillow. While you are away from home, a radio can be left playing softly in another room to offer comfort. Of course, your

puppy is going to cry at night, but don't give in. Your objective is an adult dog that is controllable at the end of a busy day and allows you to sleep at night. If you don't want to share your bed with a 45-pound dog in a year, don't allow it now while he is young.

KENNELING YOUR DOG

If it is necessary to kennel your dog, be sure to give him quality time daily. Determine from the beginning that you will share a few minutes with him each day. This can be to your advantage, too. Walking briskly to release your own pent-up frustrations is an ideal solution to an elevated blood pressure—and it's good for your heart. Talk to him as you go, and change direction intermittently so he must adjust his direction to your own. When you return home, a quick brushing of his coat will stimulate the natural oils and give your dog the pleasure of your attention. Then during the long hours when he is left alone, it would be good to provide him with safe chew toys like Nylabones® on which to vent his frustrations. Never give your dog bones from the kitchen, as they can splinter and puncture an intestine, causing death. Avoid rubber and plastic toys as well; they are often deadly when ingested.

The American Water Spaniel's curly coat is insulating and waterproof, leaving him indifferent to the frigid temperatures. Ch. Just Plain Ol' Loreley owned by John and Susan Liemohn.

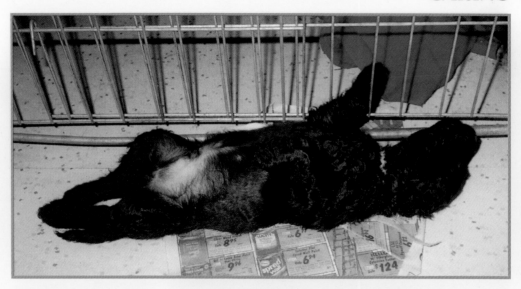

A boring environment will put your puppy right to sleep! Make sure to provide your AWS with lots of toys and a comfortable place to play.

Outdoor dogs require not only protection from the wind in foul weather but also bedding that will insulate from the cold ground. A house with a double floor (4 inches of air space), bedded with straw or cedar shavings, will allow retention of body heat. Cedar shavings offer the added advantage of repelling the incessant summer fleas.

The surface of your dog run can consist of any number of materials. The best, some say, is concrete, as it is easily washed down and disinfected. A gravel kennel is easy to clean as well, and can be replaced. The sunlight on the gravel will kill surface bacteria and worm eggs, and it can be washed with disinfectant to eliminate the sub-level pests. Concrete blocks can be set into the ground (holes up), covered with 3 inches of gravel, for better drainage. Breeders will agree that dogs raised on gravel runs develop a tighter toe structure, eliminating the fault of splayed toes.

Kennel fencing can vary, too; the easiest structure being the ready-made dog run. In the country, where there is more available space, you may want to use woven-wire fencing. Whichever choice is made, it would be wise to dig a trench, setting the fence beneath ground level 6 inches. Be aware that dogs who want to get out can do so, either digging under or climbing over. Precautions must be made to prevent their escape. Another option is the installation of electronic fencing, whereby a wire is buried beneath the surface of the ground and the dog wears a collar that will give him a twinge of current if he gets too close to it.

Shade will need to be provided during the hot summer days. A sheet of plywood or a wooden pallet can be shingled to shield from the sun as well as to repel the rain. Leaning it against the dog house or fence at a 45-degree angle should allow ample room for your dog to lie beneath it. With each end open, air circulation will allow heat to dissipate.

FEEDING

You have heard the saying, "You are what you eat." There is no breed of dog that loves his food more than the American Water Spaniel, but since he will eat nearly anything, many are not given a proper diet. The amount of food that your dog requires depends upon

Your American Water Spaniel puppy will eat just about anything, but to keep him healthy, provide him with a nutritious, well-balanced diet. Owner, Lara Suesens.

the conditions in which he lives. A kennel dog must maintain warmth during the cold winter months, so he will need a larger amount of food with added fat. Many of the commercial kibble or biscuit foods are well balanced and better able to protect your dog's health and maintain him in good condition than are table scraps. Meat should be added to the dry dog food for added protein, as well as a vitamin-mineral supplement year-round. To maintain a glossy coat, a small amount of oil should be added intermittently. There are commercial oils available for this purpose, though a quarter pat of butter will suffice.

A dog's diet should not be changed abruptly, as it will upset his digestion, and both heavy feeding or no food in his stomach may cause him to become car sick. Also, two small meals per day are better than one large one. Of course, an ample supply of fresh water is essential. Provide it at all times of year, in all kinds of weather, changing it often.

Carrots are rich in fiber, carbohydrates, and vitamin A. The Carrot Bone™ by Nylabone® is a durable chew containing no plastics or artificial ingredients and it can be served to your American Water Spaniel as-is, in a bone-hard form, or microwaved to a biscuit consistency.

KEEPING YOUR DOG SAFE

Loss of a family pet is a heartbreaking experience, and though some deaths occur unpredictably through accidents, many can be avoided. Death on the highway is probably the most common cause of animal death. Of course, there is always a threat of theft, so when your dog is off leash, he should be either under your control or confined.

Local rules on restraint and confinement, when followed, will prevent your dog from running into the path of an oncoming car. But when left alone outside for any length of time, a dog will seek an "escape"—he will either dig beneath his fenced boundary or climb over it. Yet the most threatening possibilities for loss occur while you and your dog are away from home on a trip or vacation. In this situation, his daily

The newest method of identification is the microchip, a computer chip that is no bigger than a grain of rice, that is injected into the dog's skin.

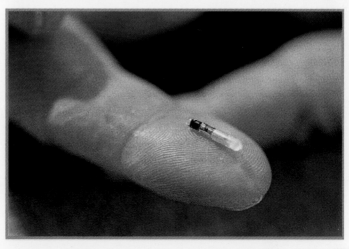

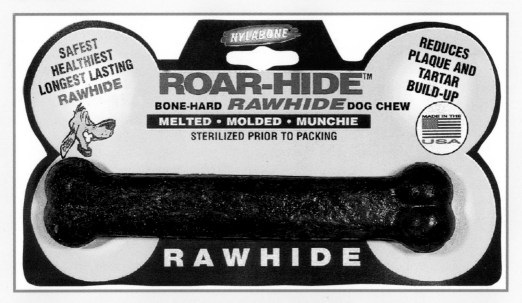

routine is greatly upset. Your attentions are else-where, and his confinement and restraint are difficult to handle. If he should wander away while left alone in a strange area, he will likely be unable to return to your car, a campsite, or Aunt Jane's house, even from around the block. His homing instinct and search for you are going to urge him to make the long trip home, which very few dogs can accomplish as well as Lassie.

Dognappers are a very real threat to dog owners across this country. Dogs that are running loose are enticed to accept a handout and nabbed.

A loving, responsible owner can take the following precautions to prevent loss:

• At your local hardware store, buy a small key ring and attach your dog's tags to it, replacing the S-curve fittings of soft aluminum. Easily snagged and bent, many tags are lost in the field, leaving a lost dog with no identification on his collar.

• By law of most communities, both a license tag and rabies tag are to be worn by your dog at all times. These numbers can be traced to you by the person who finds your dog simply by calling the veterinar-ian who administered the rabies shot (if his phone number is on the tag) or the community clerk's office, who can trace the dog license number to you.

• Order an ID tag with your complete phone number on it (and address if you wish). Don't put your dog's name on it, as it is too great an advantage for a thief.

Roar-Hide® is completely edible and is high in protein (over 86%) and low in fat (less than one-third of 1%). Unlike common rawhide, it is safer, less messy, and more fun for your American Water Spaniel.

key to unlocking his great potential. Your puppy, being young and impressionable, can become more aware, intelligent, discerning, and worldly through his experiences. You are urged to make a close companion of him by living with him, including him in your life, and allowing him to know you well. The American Water Spaniel is at his very best as a companion.

Conversely, as a kennel dog he does not excel. He will be resented by the neighbors for his barking; teased by local children when you are not at home, soon soured in disposition. When taken to the field to run after days of confinement, is it any wonder the "prisoner" applies his freedom of choice, leaving you behind? It is only with an investment of yourself, your

A cute and cuddly American Water Spaniel pup might be hard to resist, but you must seriously consider dog ownership a lifelong commitment. Owner, Lara Suesens.

time, your patience, and your interaction that you will produce an American Water Spaniel who is a companion of distinction.

MALE OR FEMALE?

Before the purchase of a puppy you should consider the eventual purpose for your dog—family pet, hunter, etc. Unless your dog develops into one of exceptional quality, she should not be bred. Although it is enticing to predict that a litter will pay for the purchase price of your female, this is seldom the case. Too often a purebred female escapes only to be serviced by the neighbor's male, leaving you with a mixed litter of puppies to sell (or give away). There are also unforeseen veterinary expenses: whelping com-

plications, caesarean sections, stillborn puppies, even the death of your beloved companion. Even when successful in your attempts, the sale of seven or more puppies at your expected price may take months instead of weeks. Any breeder can tell you that it takes months of promotion and advertising to be able to move a litter through a kennel. Local newspaper ads are not enough. Your market is nationwide. So, left with several six or seven-month-old pups to sell, you may find yourself giving pups away in desperation.

There are those among us who have preferences in male/female. Females are believed by some to be more sensitive and patient. Males can be more assertive, and are always aware of their territorial rights. They are also subject to the scent of the neighboring females in season, pacing restlessly, slipping away from home, risking death by roaming the streets freely.

If your preference is a female, then it would certainly be wise to have her spayed and avoid the frustrations of her gestation seasons twice each year. But *do not* spay her until she has been through her first season, near six months of age. If she is spayed too early, not fully matured, she will be forever immature,

At seven weeks old, this puppy is almost ready for a new home. His breeder will be looking for a responsible owner to take good care of him. Owners, John and Susan Liemohn.

insecure, and a perpetual adolescent. Allow her to reach the age of ten months before spaying her, and live with a stable, secure dog.

YOUR PUPPY'S FIRST NIGHTS

New puppies are not always cute and cuddly. Introducing one into your home will mean some changes for you and your family, so prior considerations should be made. Where will he sleep? What rooms will he be allowed in? Through what door will he be let outside to relieve himself? Who will respond to his needs? How will you keep him in your yard and off the highway? Where will he be confined while you are away from home?

Provide your American Water pup with a cozy spot to call his own in order to make him feel content and secure in his new surroundings or else he will try to find one on his own.

The behavior of a puppy and his access within a home must be controlled—for your welfare and his own. As teething and chewing are very destructive and the pup's energy level is intense, it is recommended you provide a wire dog crate in which he can spend solitary hours and sleep at night. This is not inhumane but responsible dog management, and several advantages can be gained. Housebreaking your puppy will be easier if he is confined at night. He'll try to avoid soiling the area in which he sleeps. During the day when you are unable to watch him closely, he can nap in his crate, and there is great peace of mind knowing he is not off by himself, destructively chewing on your furniture or shoes. When you are at work or away in the evening he will be safe from electrocution by chewing on a lamp cord, or from the hazardous ingestion of a plastic or rubber item that only an autopsy can reveal. If you intend to show him, the crate will be used on the show bench to restrict the attentions of people who may startle or upset your dog. And the crate will be most appreciated on hunting trips when it's time to return home with your wet, muddy dog.

Being away from mother, brothers, and sisters is a sad experience for your puppy. He will be confused and frightened, and you can expect him to howl when he is left alone. His activities will range from a flurry of activity to sporadic napping. When he is awake,

Opposite: Experiencing a loving relationship with a responsible child will help your puppy become a well-socialized dog. This is Erin Blandford with an American Water Spaniel pup.

To keep him out of trouble, give your American Water Spaniel a Nylabone®. It will keep him occupied while keeping his gums and teeth healthy.

constant supervision will prevent destructive chewing. As you know, electrical cords are most life threatening, but the loss of your favorite pair of shoes can bring you a good-sized jolt, too. So, provide a chew toy for his teething months. If you catch him chewing on something forbidden, scold him, then offer him a Gumabone® as a substitute. He'll catch on quickly enough. When he is older, provide hard Nylabones® from the pet shop, as they will keep him occupied while helping to keep his teeth and gums clean.

If you choose not to use the dog crate, there are many good dog beds available for young puppies. Make sure you place the bed in a warm, draft-free area and furnish it with a soft blanket or pillow. While you are away from home, a radio can be left playing softly in another room to offer comfort. Of course, your

Attach it to your dog's collar in addition to the other tags, but place them back to back so the engraving does not wear off them. If the jingling bothers you, glue them together with super glue or tape them together.

- Put your dog indoors if you are going to be away from home, even for a short time.
- Ask your vet about tattooing your dog. Most avid dog show and hunting enthusiasts do so, with the tattoo placed on the inside of the dog's rear leg. You could place your vet's telephone number there, or your own, if you believe you will not be moving from the area. The National Dog Registry has been organized to allow this type of identification, and they have their own numbering system. Their phone number is 1-800-NDR-DOGS. Of course, the tattoo will help you rescue your dog *only* if he has been picked up by someone other than a thief. Also, the person of rescue must know how to trace the number to you. Seek the guidance of your veterinarian, animal shelter, and law enforcement agencies.
- Microchips are available, to be placed under the skin in the shoulder area of the dog. If the dog is lost and picked up by the humane society, they can trace you by scanning the microchip.

At the time of your dog's loss, you will panic. For this reason you should have a file assembled on your dog that contains the following:

- AKC registration paper and pedigree.

POPpups™ are 100% edible and enhanced with dog-friendly ingredients like liver, cheese, spinach, chicken, carrots, or potatoes. They contain no salt, sugar, alcohol, plastic or preservatives. You can even microwave a POPpup™ to turn into a huge crackly treat for your American Water Spaniel.

His inquisitive nature and curiosity about the outside world may cause your puppy to go wandering off, so always supervise him closely when he is outside. Owner, Paul Morrison.

• Rabies certificate from the administering veterinarian.
• Dog license of your township or community, which is has an assigned number.
• Inoculation record from your veterinarian.
In addition to the above it is wise to include:
• Clear, sharp photos of your dog (head alone, side, and front). Include the negatives of these shots in a sealed plastic bag in case you wish to have several prints made.
• A written description of your dog (any scars that he may have; individual identifying marks, i.e., white spot on chest or toes; height; and weight).
• Phone numbers of your local dog pound, humane rescue organizations, police, animal control office, and newspaper classified lost and found phone number.

To avoid the heartache of losing your dog, keep your American Water on lead at all times when outdoors. Owner, Lara Suesens.

The nightmare begins like this. You arrive home, or simply step outside, and find your dog is missing and doesn't respond to your calls. It is natural to deny it, thinking that he'll be home for dinner. Don't waste time. Call on neighbors with a photo of your dog in hand. Send the kids with a photo to ask at other houses down the street. Ask the mailman and the paper boy to watch for him. Then, calmly do the following:

• Make up a flier with a photo of your dog on it, or any picture of an American Water Spaniel. Don't include the name of your dog, as it is an advantage

A fenced-in yard is a perfect way to protect your American Water Spaniel from becoming lost or stolen.

for one who has found and intends to keep him. And in case the dog has not yet been nabbed, it would be an advantage for the nabbers to use his name to catch him. Add your phone number as a contact, and if you feel it might help, offer a reward.

• Call animal shelters and make certain they understand what an American Water Spaniel looks like. Send or take one of your fliers to them.

• Call local veterinarians to ask if they have treated an AWS for injury recently and describe the breed to them. Not all vets are familiar with the breed. Take a flier to them later.

- Place the fliers you have created in coin laundries, grocery stores, convenience stores, and churches. Give some to children to post at school; take some to the humane society or pound. Put them in highly visible places in your area (businesses and restaurants).
- Call your local newspapers and place a lost ad (omitting your dog's name), describing him as: "Lost: Medium-sized, brown, curly spaniel. Call (your phone number)."

This author has on at least four occasions taken in stray dogs until their owners could be located. Only one of them wore an appropriate ID tag, and still it took nearly a full day to get the owner on the phone. In three

Opposite: Know the whereabouts of your dog at all times, especially in the field where unfamiliar surroundings or sounds might confuse your American Water Spaniel.

It's a big world out there, so make sure your American Water Spaniel always wears his collar and tags in case he should become separated from you. Ch. Waterway's Bodee-O-Do, WDX owned by John and Linda Hattrem.

instances, the owners were eventually located through the awareness of our paper boy. In the last case, the dog had traveled outside the paper route and it took an ad in the classifieds and a full week to locate the grateful owner.

To avoid heartache, keep your dog under control and make sure he is identified at all times.

BREED RESCUE

If circumstances should occur which necessitate giving up your dog, you are encouraged to contact the breeder from whom you purchased him. It may be possible to place the dog within a loving home immediately. The American Water Spaniel Club has a

Your American Water Spaniel is a valued family member. This is UKC/AKC Ch. U-CDX Little Brownies Cinnamon Teal, CDX, JWD owned by Paul and Lynn Morrison. From field to show— this dog has done it all!

rescue committee which can be reached by calling 1-800-555-AWSC. Also, The American Water Spaniel Field Association, Inc. can be located at P.O. 160, Union Lake, Michigan 48387-0160 to offer assistance by their rescue committee. Please don't drop the dog off at the dog pound or give him to a friend who will not value him. A volunteer foster home may be able to care for him until a permanent home can be found, enabling him to live out his remaining years with dignity and love. And if you are in a position to donate a loving effort to the placement of unwanted American Waters, these rescue committees would like to hear from you.

GROOMING YOUR AMERICAN WATER SPANIEL

The tools necessary for grooming this breed are not expensive. A firm bristle brush will remove shedding coat and distribute coat oils uniformly. This can become "quality time" spent with your dog. A comb will be needed for the feathering on his legs and tail. However, you will not be able to comb out the collections of burrs that have matted together after a hard day in the field. With patience, they can be removed by hand, spreading the hair from the burr (versus pulling the burr from the hair). Grooming your dog will be easier if he has first been allowed to run and stretch his legs.

If you accustom your American Water Spaniel to regular grooming procedures at an early age, he will come to think of it as a pleasurable experience. These pups are becoming used to the height of the grooming table. Owners, Paul and Lynn Morrison.

Although the hair on your dog will not grow to great lengths, he will likely develop shaggy, unruly hairs. A pair of blunt-nosed scissors can be used safely. The straggly hair atop his head can be removed by first brushing the hair in the opposite direction (toward his nose) to get it to stand up above the rest. With the scissor blades pointing toward the back of your dog's head, press them down firmly onto his head and slowly cut. Then, smooth the hair back into place.

Only light trimming of the ears will be necessary unless you wish to shorten the hair for the hunting season. To trim the ragged locks, use the scissors, cutting in the direction the hair is laying. The hair

Spaniels are prone to ear problems because of their long and heavy ears. Be sure to keep your American Water's ears clean and free of waxy build-up. Owner, Lara Suesens.

surrounding the ear opening should be removed and kept short to allow for evaporation of moisture within the ear (preventing sores).

The feathering on his feet will need to be trimmed closely, and scissors can also be used for this purpose if you have no clippers. Brush the hair upward, so that it stands up, and cut it in the direction toward the toes. Remove the excess hair between his toes and on the bottom around the pads, leaving a smoothly-shaped foot. Trimming toenails, if done regularly from youth, will not become a difficult task, though your dog may not like the clicking sound of the cut. Toenail clippers can be found at a pet shop. Use great caution when cutting. One painful, careless cut to the quick will forever be remembered by your dog and from that day forward your grooming will be done with difficulty.

Bathing an American Water Spaniel is quite easy. Purchase a good, anti-bacterial dog shampoo from your pet shop. Other soaps may irritate his skin and damage his coat. Application is best accomplished if the shampoo is diluted a bit with water. In the summertime, bathing can be easily done with the garden hose. Tie the dog securely to a tree or post and wet him thoroughly. Dispense a ring of shampoo around his neck, just behind the ears (to prevent any fleas from hiding in his ears), and encircle his tail as well. Lather him well, avoiding the eyes and nose. Then rinse him thoroughly, rubbing as you apply the water. When finished, you can turn him loose to run, making sure he will not leave your yard, as great enthusiasm will be shown.

Daily brushing of your American Water's coat will prevent heavy shedding and keep it free of mats.

During the cold months of the year the bath will not be as much fun. The laundry tub or bathtub can be used, wetting him by pouring water over him from a plastic container. When you are finished, wrap him in a towel to absorb the excess moisture. Then, pin a dry towel about him to prevent chilling him.

A puppy's first bath is very important. Frightened dogs are very difficult to bathe, so care should be taken not to scare him. In the slippery tub he will need secure footing. Place a towel for him to stand on in the bottom of the tub. Test the water with your wrist or elbow to be sure it's not too hot. Talk soothingly to your pup as you begin pouring the water over his back. The noises will be unfamiliar to him, and loud in a tiled room. An assistant can be of tremendous help.

Cleaning your dog's ears will be required if you are to prevent ear canker. Spaniels are prone to retention of moisture in the ear, allowing the growth of irritants and mites. Trimming the excess hair around the opening of the ear may prevent a problem by allowing the moisture to evaporate. As with the other treatments, this will never become difficult if you begin properly and avoid hurting him. The area you want to clean is a channel directly down his neck (or near the surface of his skin). With a paper towel wrapped about your small finger you will be able to reach down, absorbing some of the moisture. Cotton-tipped wipes can be used (with care), aided by a flashlight, to better see into the ear. If the ear appears red, professional aid and medication should be sought. A condition of the eye, ear, or skin can develop into a serious affliction in a very short time. Don't neglect them.

Your American Water Spaniel is exposed to many dangers in the field, including thorns, burrs and parasites. Be sure to check his coat thoroughly after working or playing outdoors.

FIELD TRAINING

PREPARATION

Gunshyness is not a hereditary trait, but some dogs tend to be more fearful and shy. Therefore, offspring of these dogs may inherit this same fearful temperament. But if young puppies are accustomed to loud noises in their first few weeks of life, the problem of gunshyness may never develop. Gunshyness is the scourge of the hunting world, and with a little effort, can be prevented. A knowledgeable breeder will have

Introduce your American Water Spaniel to the field gradually, making sure his first experiences are positive ones. Wildmoor's Copenhagen, WD at a hunt test with owner Erik Wahlstrom.

accustomed the puppies in a litter to a reasonable level of noise at meal time.

Loud banging at feeding time can accustom your puppy to loud noises. Make certain he is deeply engrossed in his dinner. You could keep a hammer handy for the resetting of nails on his house, or simply rap a small pan lid upon the fence. Be attentive, though, as the object is to prevent him from being frightened in the future, not scaring the spirit out of him now.

47

When you feed your puppy, stay near him as he eats and make light banging noises, increasing the volume over time. Watch for his reaction, though, and try to do this when he is fully engrossed in his dinner. When he is a little older, you can fire a cap pistol at a distance during mealtimes. Introduction of the shotgun should be done with caution. Shooting over a young, inexperienced dog can be greatly damaging, creating the gunshyness that one wishes to avoid. When your dog is fired over at close range for the first time, it is important that the dog be working a fresh scent and that the bird be brought down to enhance his experience. Aim well.

American Water Spaniel pups have the "nose" for game. Acclimating your American Water Spaniel to the scents of the field will make him more receptive to training exercises.

HUNTING BY NOSE

The use of his nose will come naturally to your American Water, though he will not at first know what game he is tracking. Take him at an early age into the open field. For this purpose he should be wearing a leather or nylon collar with an ID tag attached that contains your phone number or your address. A whistle should be about your neck, ready to call to him in with repeated bursts when his range becomes too

Opposite: Ch. Choco Lot Morrison, CDX and Ch. Little Brownies Gunner Boy, CD with owner Paul Morrison following a Michigan pheasant hunt.

48

great. It is assumed that you have worked with him at home in your yard, he knows his name, and you have developed a companionship. Never take a newly purchased dog out off lead and expect him to come back to you. If you doubt that he will stay with you, a lightweight check line can be used in open meadows. This will restrain him, training him to stay within an acceptable range.

Introducing your young dog to the game of the field can best be done early in the morning while the scent of game lingers on dew-covered grass. As he is your companion, he will be grateful that you introduced him to the wonderful world of birds. To change direction, seeking a hedge row or other cover where the birds will be found, call him by name to get his attention, and at the same time, turn and step off in another direction. Raise your arm to signal to him, as if you were throwing in the direction you wish him to go. This will acquaint him with hand signals. Don't expect him to consider you "leader" if you try to call him off a bird. Watch for his tail action; it will whip with excitement as the game becomes nearer.

INTRODUCTION TO WATER

Your pup's introduction to water can be enjoyable for both of you during the summer months, as the breed has a natural affinity for water. If he is very

With an air of pride and competence, Scooter waits beside his retrieves on a crisp South Dakota morning. Owners, Karen and Steve Rodock.

American Water Spaniels have an affinity for the water and are innate retrievers. Ch. Just Plain Ol' Lucy and Ch. Just Plain Ol' Molly Brown, CDX bring a bumper back to shore.

young, take care not to frighten him. Allow him time to discover his natural abilities.

At first, allow him to walk about the shoreline and play. Toss small twigs into the water near him so that he can walk out to get them. Then, when he is more comfortable in shallow water, encourage him to step out into deeper water. He will discover that he can swim. If possible, swim with him. You will be sharing the pleasure of his new experience, and it will enhance your bond. Notice the use of his tail as a rudder when he changes direction. He is also utilizing the webbed toes of each foot to increase the power of his stroke.

When you toss sticks for him to retrieve, use his name followed by the command "Fetch." Lengthen

Ch. Just Plain Ol' Molly Brown, CDX owned by John and Sue Liemohn leaps into Cedar Creek in Anoka, Minnesota.

the retrieves, being careful not to discourage him. Remember that his perspective across the surface of the water is not as good as yours while you are standing on shore. Never insensitively throw him into the water. Don't press him beyond his capability.

Foster your American Water pup's retrieving instincts by playing games like "fetch." This pup has fun while returning the retrieving dummy to his watchful master.

RETRIEVING

To begin your retriever training you can introduce your dog to the dummy by teasing him with it, getting him fairly frantic to get it away from you. When this has been accomplished, toss it out in front of you a short distance. Undoubtedly he will go after it and when he

Ch. Just Plain Ol' Lucy proudly brings back her first pigeon at seven weeks of age. Owners, John and Sue Liemohn.

reaches it, begin blowing the whistle in short blasts, coaxing him back to you. If he does not come directly back, toot, toot, toot, briskly on the whistle and run in the opposite direction (away from him). The idea is to get him to chase after you until he catches up to you, then immediately take the dummy from him. If he is very young, don't require him to sit and hold the dummy. You don't want to take all of the fun out of his play. Soon, when you begin the retrieve, you can hold him lightly by the collar to delay him, then release him when the dummy is in the air. Before he leaves your side and as the dummy is at its peak say, "(dog's

John Liemohn and his American Water, Just Plain Ol' Son Of A Gun, hunting geese in North Dakota.

name), Fetch." In the course of training you should increase the distance that the dummy is being thrown but mix it occasionally with a short retrieve to keep him from anticipating the fall.

When a retriever "takes a line," he is going out in the direction that he was sent without knowing where the dummy has fallen. In order to teach this, you will need a helper to throw the dummy for you while you handle your dog. Choose a place to work where the grass is short and the dummy will be easily seen. Hold him lightly by the collar and require him to sit at the heeling position. Have your helper throw the dummy and, while it is still in the air, send your dog out using his name and the command "Fetch." Seeing the falling dummy, he of course knows where it is going to be found. When he has the dummy in his mouth, sound short toots on your whistle and coax him to bring the dummy to you. Try to get it from him before he drops it at your feet. If he appears to be ready to run away from you with it, whistle and begin running in another

Hunting spaniels need to be taught to gently give their prey to their master after retrieval. Charlie Shoulders teaches Scrapper to give him the retrieve before dropping it.

Praise and attention will encourage your American Water Spaniel to work happily and eagerly at any task you give him.

These American Water Spaniels have combined their abilities and skills for a successful day in the field.

direction so he must chase you in order to give it to you. Again, as he comes toward you, try to intercept him, running backward if necessary and coaxing until he aligns in front of you. Quickly take the dummy before he drops it. Attempt to get him to associate your swinging arm (the back of your hand beside his right ear) as a signal to the direction of the dummy. In time, when you gesture, he will turn his head and zero in on that area to which you have pointed. When he is working well on the retrieving, you can have your helper introduce the blank gun.

Ch. Little Brownie's Gunner Boy CD retrieves a live pheasant from a Michigan field. Owners, Lynn and Paul Morrison.

INDIFFERENCE

Expect to face times when your dog shows little interest in pleasing you with his retrieve. If you have tried to stimulate his interest in retrieving by teasing him with the dummy and he still shows no interest, put him back in his kennel and discontinue the lessons for a day or so. It is surprising what his attitude will be the next time he is sent after the dummy. If that still doesn't work, see if you can find someone to work his dog while your dog watches. This bit of competition should adjust his attitude.

STEADINESS

When your dog is retrieving well, running out and back at a good speed, you can begin to teach him to hold. Begin with short retrieves and make him stay only for a count of five after the dummy hits the ground. Hold him by the collar in order to prevent him from dashing out to retrieve before you give the command. When he begins to break, tell him "Sit" and put him right back in the very same spot. Stop him before he gets to the dummy, then throw it again. When he sees that he cannot retrieve it on his own, he will accept the fact that he must wait for your command.

You are urged to purchase a gun dog or a retriever training manual for more intensive field training.

TRAINING YOUR AMERICAN WATER SPANIEL

THE PSYCHOLOGY OF DOG TRAINING

The psychology of dog behavior should be understood before you begin life with your new dog. Though it has been stated that dogs are not capable of thinking, any dog owner can tell you that dogs are smart enough to take the path of least resistance. The horse, much less intelligent than the dog, can be trained by repetition and submits through habit to become relatively predictable in behavior. The cat, only one degree lower on the intelligence scale than the dog, is certainly intelligent enough, but lacks the willingness to please that is required for performance. The dog, of sufficient intelligence, may know how to

The American Water Spaniel is an easily trained breed that is always eager to please his master.

perform an act, may have repeatedly accomplished it, and yet, may look you in the eye and flatly refuse to grant you satisfaction. What must be developed and utilized is a willingness to please; the American Water generally possesses more than an ample amount, which can be greatly enhanced by the dog's relationship with his handler. This relationship of dog and handler is the primary element of trainability and must be consistently nurtured and maintained.

The dog must respect you as his leader. You provide food for him, you plan excursions of fun and

stimulation. You allow him to expand his knowledge and expertise, and you grant him the affection of a pal. But further, you retain the upper hand, and he knows that if he does not conform to your expectations, he has lost favor. That is the element with which we capture his good performance. The dog must want to please out of respect for you, his leader.

At three months, this pup is at a perfect age to begin basic obedience training.

We cannot wait until the dog is doing something wrong, ignoring him while he is performing well. It must be the reverse. More time must be spent in praise, less in correction. Not so easy, you say, but applied as a preventive measure, it is the road to good

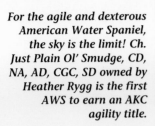

For the agile and dexterous American Water Spaniel, the sky is the limit! Ch. Just Plain Ol' Smudge, CD, NA, AD, CGC, SD owned by Heather Rygg is the first AWS to earn an AKC agility title.

performance. The dog wants to please you if your relationship with him is good, but training cannot be effective if it is considered "work" by either of you. Lightness and playfulness are much more beneficial in training your dog than heavy-handed lessons. While the dog is still young he is willing to absorb training. As an adolescent, he will be less pliable, and will want to challenge your leadership. Training a young puppy becomes an evolutionary process by which you build upon a previous lesson.

In physical training, we will attempt to manipulate the dog into doing what we wish, using vocal praise and inserting a simple command that he will recognize. Tell him to "Sit," and put him in that position (followed by petting with *praise, praise, praise*). Say "Down" and put him there. After a minute, release him from the "Down" position with a pat on your left leg as a signal, and more *praise, praise, praise*.

The voice is an underestimated tool in dog training. Through inflection of your voice alone, you can bring about animated responses from a dog. By raising the tone (mocking baby-talk in a falsetto tone) you can bring about an eager playfulness in a dog. It exudes lightness and is playful.

Remember, training a dog is not really easy. At first he doesn't know what you wish. Soon, he will know, and for a while he will want to do it for you. But the day will come when he simply challenges your right to command and asserts his right to refuse. The first time it happens, you might give him the benefit of the doubt. Did he understand the command? Was he distracted by his surroundings? If he is challenging you, he will fail to respond the second time. Then you can conclude it is clearly defiance. You must now let him know that you are not asking, but commanding him to perform. Repeat the command, louder and more forcefully, and, if he refuses, physically guide him through the required action. Now, even though he didn't act as commanded, praise him lavishly, as though there had been no correction. If you are too soft or inconsistent in your responses, allowing him to disobey, your future commands will be taken lightly, or worse, disregarded.

A good dog trainer knows when to start and when to quit a training session. He never attempts to train or work his dog when he is himself out of sorts. In relating well with a dog, you will be able to read him and know his state of being, and your perception will measure the dog's willingness to please. And you can be sure that he reads you, too. A yawning dog displays a lack of interest. A disobedient, defiant one may be telling you to quit before your patience is lost. But don't end a lesson on a sour note. Always leave the training session after the successful execution of a command. We certainly don't want a disobedient dog to force us to quit training him. Choose a simple lesson that he can do

Ch. Sweet Raisin No Ruckus, CD shown by owner Rick Butler winning Group Four.

well, and praise him lavishly when he completes it. Then romp about with him playfully.

Sadly, dog training is never done. It is the result of an ongoing relationship between an intelligent animal and yourself. And, perhaps, if we did not underestimate the intelligence of our dogs, we might better be able to hold their interest. Learning, then, can be a continual process throughout his life. But, repetition is insulting to a trained dog. When he knows the lesson, and must repeatedly perform it in the same old way, is it any wonder his expression reflects the question, "Why?"

To hold his interest (reflected in his enthusiasm), the pattern of the lessons and training must move quickly and be altered in sequence. You must keep

Agility trials allow the American Water Spaniel to apply his natural abilities to the competition ring. Little Brownies Lady Heidi owned by Margaret Will.

him guessing, remembering that he is not a machine that is forever programmed to perform. Varying the lessons and allowing him something new to learn will increase his want of learning. Your success will show in his attitude; your interactions or performances together will reveal your relationship with your dog. Stay ahead of him with praise, intuition to prevent his error, or a sharp "No!" correction when he refuses, followed immediately by praise for your wonderful dog.

This book is not intended to be the solution to all your training questions. There are many good books

on training, written by professional handlers, that describe the results that can be effected from specific training situations or how to alleviate any handling problems.

Young puppies may become bored or tired easily, so keep training sessions short and fun!

HOUSEBREAKING YOUR PUPPY

The easiest way to housebreak your puppy is to restrict the space in which he moves. Confinement at night in the dog crate will be a tremendous aid, as he will at an early age avoid soiling his bed. Take him out to do his business as soon as he awakes from napping, as well as the first thing in the morning. Immediately after eating, you will notice him circling frantically with his nose to the floor, seeking the proper spot. Quickly get him outside. Take him by the collar or call him by name as you rush to the door, saying "Out." Leaving a leash attached to his collar may aid you in guiding him quickly to the door.

If you notice him sniffing at the floor in quick little steps, get him outside quickly. If possible, it should always be the same door so he develops the habit of seeking that door when he wants to go outside.

BREAKING TO COLLAR AND LEAD

Begin by placing a lightweight collar on your puppy. The nylon ones are comfortable and inexpensive, though it will soon become outgrown and need to be replaced. At first your puppy will be distressed by the feel of the collar around his neck. After he has settled down and accepted it, attach a light leash (lead) to the collar and let it drag about behind your puppy. This will allow him to adjust to the weight of it before you begin to use pressure or restraint. Intermittently call to him, using his name and pulling lightly on the lead. Always extend lavish praise each time he comes to you. When you begin walking him on lead, keep him beside your left leg, as that is the proper heeling position.

The time to create a well-mannered dog is when he is young. "No" can be easily understood and respected at an early age. He will, however, only respect you if you are firm and consistent with correction and praise. The first time you witness your puppy chewing on something forbidden, it is time to correct him. Raising your voice a bit, say "No!"

Teaching your dog to wear his leash and collar is necessary and will come in handy in many different situations, including the field. George Christiansen with Beau's Nighthawk Ruff Rider, WD.

Immediately after correction you must compensate with loving praise and affection. Speak encouragingly to him, pat him, hug him, and let him know that correction time is past. The act is forgiven, you are friends again.

To adjust your dog's behavior it is essential that he be corrected while in the act of doing wrong or immediately afterward. If minutes have elapsed and the situation changes, he will not know what he did or why he is being corrected. A mistake brings a sharp "No" correction followed by praise encourages him to do right. Better yet, prevent his error. This requires anticipating his next action, reacting quickly to divert him into performing as desired, which is the ultimate in dog handling.

Never chase your dog in an attempt to correct him, allowing him to avoid you. Never call your dog to you to correct him. When he responds to his name and comes to you he must always be rewarded with praise, acceptance and love. And last, never issue a command you cannot enforce.

Ch. Countrysids Happy Hiram is a two-time Westminster Kennel Club Best of Breed winner and a top-producing sire of five champions. Owner-handled by Barbara Spisak.

THE COME COMMAND

Come is the most vital of all commands and especially so for the independently minded dog. To teach the puppy to come, let him reach the end of a long lead, then give the command and his name, gently pulling him toward you at the same time. As soon as he associates the word come with the action of moving toward you, pull only when he does not respond immediately. As he starts to come, move back to make him learn that he must come from a distance as well as when he is close to you. Soon you may be able to practice without a leash, but if he is slow to come or notably disobedient, go to him and

Versatility is one reason the American Water Spaniel appeals to many people. This AWS clears the solid jump in the Open class at an AWSC, Inc. match.

pull him toward you, repeating the command. Never scold a dog during this exercise—or any other exercise. Remember the trick is that the puppy must want to come to you. For the very independent dog, hand signals may work better than verbal commands.

THE SIT COMMAND

As with most basic commands, your puppy will learn this one in just a few lessons. You can give the puppy two lessons a day on the sit command but he will make just as much progress with one 15-minute lesson each day. Some trainers will advise you that you should not proceed to other commands until the previous one has been learned really well. However, a bright young pup is quite capable of handling more than one command per lesson, and certainly per day. Indeed, as time progresses, you will be going through each command as a matter of routine before a new one is attempted. This is so the puppy always starts, as well as ends, a lesson on a high note, having successfully completed something.

Call the puppy to you and fuss over him. Place one hand on his hindquarters and the other under his upper chest. Say "Sit" in a pleasant (never harsh) voice. At the same time, push down his rear end and

Little Brownies Lady Heidi sails through the tire jump at an agility demonstration. Owner, Margaret Will.

push up under his chest. Now lavish praise on the puppy. Repeat this a few times and your pet will get the idea. Once the puppy is in the sit position you will release your hands. At first he will tend to get up, so immediately repeat the exercise. The lesson will end when the pup is in the sit position. When the puppy understands the command, and does it right away, you can slowly move backwards so that you are a few feet away from him. If he attempts to come to you, simply place him back in the original position and start again. Do not attempt to keep the pup in the sit position for too long. At this age, even a few seconds is a long while and you do not want him to get bored with lessons before he has even begun them.

All dogs should be able to walk beside their owner without pulling. Ch. Just Plain Ol' Jake, CD demonstrates heeling with owner Sue Liemohn.

THE HEEL COMMAND

All dogs should be able to walk nicely on a leash without their owners being involved in a tug-of-war. The heel command will follow leash training. Heel training is best done where you have a wall to one side of you. This will restrict the puppy's lateral movements, so you only have to contend with forward and backward situations. A fence is an alternative, or you can do the lesson in the garage. Again, it is better to do the lesson in private, not on a public sidewalk where there will be many distractions.

With a puppy, there will be no need to use a choke collar as you can be just as effective with a regular one. The leash should be of good length, certainly not too short. You can adjust the space between you, the puppy, and the wall so your pet has only a small amount of room to move sideways. This being so, he will either hang back or pull ahead—the latter is the more desirable state as it indicates a bold pup who is not frightened of you.

Hold the leash in your right hand and pass it through your left. As the puppy moves ahead and strains on the leash, give the leash a quick jerk backwards with your left hand, at the same time saying "Heel." The position you want the pup to be in is such that his chest

67

is level with, or just behind, an imaginary line from your knee. When the puppy is in this position, praise him and begin walking again, and the whole exercise will be repeated. Once the puppy begins to get the message, you can use your left hand to pat the side of your knee so the pup is encouraged to keep close to your side.

American Water Spaniel Ch. Just Plain Ol' Smudge owned by Heather Rygg became the first of his breed to earn a USDAA agility title.

It is useful to suddenly do an about-turn when the pup understands the basics. The puppy will now be behind you, so you can pat your knee and say "Heel." As soon as the pup is in the correct position, give him lots of praise. The puppy will now be beginning to associate certain words with certain actions. Whenever he is not in the heel position he will experience displeasure as you jerk the leash, but when he comes alongside you he will receive praise. Given these two options, he will always prefer the latter—assuming he has no other reason to fear you, which would then create a dilemma in his mind.

Once the lesson has been well learned, then you can adjust your pace from a slow walk to a quick one and the puppy will come to adjust. The slow walk is always the more difficult for most puppies, as they are usually anxious to be on the move.

If you have no wall to walk against then things will be a little more difficult because the pup will tend to wander to his left. This means you need to give lateral

68

jerks as well as bring the pup to your side. End the lesson when the pup is walking nicely beside you. Begin the lesson with a few sit commands (which he understands by now), so you're starting with success and praise. If your puppy is nervous on the leash, you should never drag him to your side as you may see so many other people do (who obviously didn't invest in a good book like you did!). If the pup sits down, call him to your side and give lots of praise. The pup must always come to you because he wants to. If he is dragged to your side he will see you doing the dragging—a big negative. When he races ahead he does not see you jerk the leash, so all he knows is that something restricted his movement and, once he was in a given position, you gave him lots of praise. This is using canine psychology to your advantage.

Always try to remember that if a dog must be disciplined, then try not to let him associate the discipline with you. This is not possible in all matters but, where it is, this is definitely to be preferred.

THE STAY COMMAND

This command follows from the sit. Face the puppy and say "Sit." Now step backwards, and as you do,

A well-trained American Water Spaniel will know how to behave in any situation. This pup shows restraint and discipline with this eager toddler.

say "Stay." Let the pup remain in the position for only a few seconds before calling him to you and giving lots of praise. Repeat this, but step further back. You do not need to shout at the puppy. Your pet is not deaf; in fact, his hearing is far better than yours. Speak just loudly enough for the pup to hear, yet use a firm voice. You can stretch the word to form a "sta-a-a-y." If the pup gets up and comes to you simply lift him up, place

him back in the original position, and start again. As the pup comes to understand the command, you can move further and further back.

Ch. Waterway's Bodee-O-Do, WDX owned by John and Linda Hattrem wins Second in Group.

The next test is to walk away after placing the pup. This will mean your back is to him, which will tempt him to follow you. Keep an eye over your shoulder, and the minute the pup starts to move, spin around and, using a sterner voice, say either "Sit" or "Stay." If the pup has gotten quite close to you, then, again, return him to the original position.

As the weeks go by you can increase the length of time the pup is left in the stay position—but two to

If you wish to bring your American Water Spaniel along on trips, make sure he is accustomed to his crate. It is the safest way for him to travel.

three minutes is quite long enough for a puppy. If your puppy drops into a lying position and is clearly more comfortable, there is nothing wrong with this. Likewise, your pup will want to face the direction in which you walked off. Some trainers will insist that the dog faces the direction he was placed in, regardless of whether you move off on his blind side. I have never believed in this sort of obedience because it has no practical benefit.

THE DOWN COMMAND

From the puppy's viewpoint, the down command can be one of the more difficult ones to accept. This is because the position is one taken up by a submissive dog in a wild pack situation. A timid dog will roll over—a natural gesture of submission. A bolder pup will want to get up, and might back off, not feeling he should have to submit to this command. He will feel that he is under attack from you and about to be punished—which is what would be the position in his natural environment. Once he comes to understand this is not the case, he will accept this unnatural position without any problem.

You may notice that some dogs will sit very quickly, but will respond to the down command more slowly—it is their way of saying that they will obey the command, but under protest!

There two ways to teach this command. One is, in my mind, more intimidating than the other, but it is up to you to decide which one works best for you. The first method is to stand in front of your puppy and bring him to the sit position, with his collar and leash on. Pass the leash under your left foot so that when you pull on it, the result is that the pup's neck is forced downwards. With your free left hand, push the pup's shoulders down while at the same time saying "Down."

Eight-year old Ch. Just Plain Ol' Lucy shown by owner Sue Liemohn taking Best of Opposite Sex in the Veterans Class at an American Spaniel Club Show.

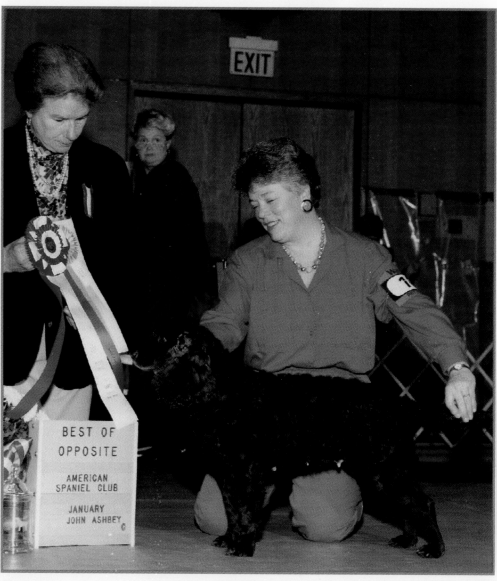

This is when a bold pup will instantly try to back off and wriggle in full protest. Hold the pup firmly by the shoulders so he stays in the position for a second or two, then tell him what a good dog he is and give him lots of praise. Repeat this only a few times in a lesson because otherwise the puppy will get bored and upset over this command. End with an easy command that brings back the pup's confidence.

The second method, and the one I prefer, is done as follows: Stand in front of the pup and then tell him to sit. Now kneel down, which is immediately far less intimidating to the puppy than to have you towering above him. Take each of his front legs and pull them

Your AWS puppy will look to you, his owner, for the direction and discipline he needs to be a well-mannered pet.

forward, at the same time saying "Down." Release the legs and quickly apply light pressure on the shoulders with your left hand. Then, as quickly, say "Good boy" and give lots of fuss. Repeat two or three times only. The pup will learn over a few lessons. Remember, this is a very submissive act on the pup's behalf, so there is no need to rush matters.

RECALL TO HEEL COMMAND

When your puppy is coming to the heel position from an off-leash situation—such as if he has been running free—he should do this in the correct manner. He should pass behind you and take up his position and then sit. To teach this command, have the pup in front of you in the

73

sit position with his collar and leash on. Hold the leash in your right hand. Give him the command to heel, and pat your left knee. As the pup starts to move forward, use your right hand to guide him behind you. If need be you can hold his collar and walk the dog around the back of you to the desired position. You will need to repeat this a few times until the dog understands what is wanted.

When he has done this a number of times, you can try it without the collar and leash. If the pup comes up toward your left side, then bring him to the sit position in front of you, hold his collar and walk him around the back of you. He will eventually understand and automatically pass around your back each time. If the dog is already behind you when you recall him, then he should automatically come to your left side, which you will be patting with your hand.

Opposite: A well-trained American Water Spaniel is a pleasure to own and will be a loyal friend as well as an able hunting companion. Ch. Just Plain Ol' Molly Brown owned by John and Sue Liemohn.

THE NO COMMAND

This is a command that must be obeyed every time without fail. There are no halfway stages, he must be 100-percent reliable. Most delinquent dogs have never been taught this command; included in these are the jumpers, the barkers, and the biters. Were your puppy to approach a poisonous snake or any other potential danger, the no command, coupled with the recall, could save his life. You do not need to give a specific lesson for this command because it will crop up time and again in day-to-day life.

If the puppy is chewing a slipper, you should approach the pup, take hold of the slipper, and say "No" in a stern voice. If he jumps onto the furniture, lift him off and say "No" and place him gently on the floor. You must be consistent in the use of the command and apply it every time he is doing something you do not want him to do.

Ch. Little Brownies Lady Heidi is the first American Water Spaniel to earn a Flyball Dog Champion title.

YOUR HEALTHY AMERICAN WATER SPANIEL

Dogs, like all other animals, are capable of contracting problems and diseases that, in most cases, are easily avoided by sound husbandry—meaning well-bred and well-cared-for animals are less prone to developing diseases and problems than are carelessly bred and neglected animals. Your knowledge of how to avoid problems is far more valuable than all of the books and advice on how to cure them. Respectively, the only person you should listen to about treatment is your vet. Veterinarians don't have all the answers, but at least they are trained to analyze and treat illnesses, and are aware of the full implications of treatments. This does not mean a few old remedies aren't good standbys when all else fails, but in most cases modern science provides the best treatments for disease.

Opposite: Genetic diseases in the American Water Spaniel can be passed from generation to generation. It is important to provide preventive health care and screenings to ensure healthy animals.

PHYSICAL EXAMS

Your puppy should receive regular physical examinations or check-ups. These come in two forms. One is obviously performed by your vet, and the other is a day-to-day procedure that should be done by you. Apart from the fact the exam will highlight any problem at an early stage, it is an excellent way of socializing the pup to being handled.

To do the physical exam yourself, start at the head and work your way around the body. You are looking for any sign of lesions, or any indication of parasites on the pup. The most common parasites are fleas and ticks.

76

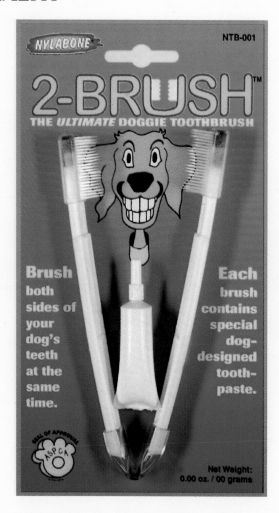

As a pet owner, it is essential to keep your dog's teeth clean by removing surface tartar and plaque. 2-Brush™ by Nylabone® is made with two toothbrushes to clean both sides of your dog's teeth at the same time. Each brush contains a toothpaste reservoir designed to apply the toothpaste, which is specially formulated for dogs, directly into the brush.

HEALTHY TEETH AND GUMS

Chewing is instinctual. Puppies chew so that their teeth and jaws grow strong and healthy as they develop. As the permanent teeth begin to emerge, it is painful and annoying to the puppy, and puppy owners must recognize that their new charges need something safe upon which to chew. Unfortunately, once the puppy's permanent teeth have emerged and settled solidly into the jaw, the chewing instinct does not fade. Adult dogs instinctively need to clean their teeth, massage their gums, and exercise their jaws through chewing.

It is necessary for your dog to have clean teeth. You should take your dog to the veterinarian at least once a year to have his teeth cleaned and to have his mouth examined for any sign of oral disease. Although dogs do not get cavities in the same way humans do, dogs'

The Hercules® by Nylabone® has raised dental tips that help fight plaque on your American Water Spaniel's teeth and gums.

teeth accumulate tartar, and more quickly than humans do! Veterinarians recommend brushing your dog's teeth daily. But who can find time to brush their dog's teeth daily? The accumulation of tartar and plaque on our dog's teeth when not removed can cause irritation and eventually erode the enamel and finally destroy the teeth. Advanced cases, while destroying the teeth, bring on gingivitis and periodontitis, two very serious conditions that can affect the dog's internal organs as well...to say nothing about bad breath!

Since everyone can't brush their dog's teeth daily or get to the veterinarian often enough for him to scale

Nylafloss® does wonders for your American Water Spaniel's dental health by massaging his gums and literally flossing between his teeth, loosening plaque and tartar build-up. Unlike cotton tug toys, Nylafloss® is made of nylon and won't rot or fray.

the dog's teeth, providing the dog with something safe to chew on will help maintain oral hygeine. Chew devices from Nylabone® keep dogs' teeth clean, but they also provide an excellent resource for entertainment and relief of doggie tensions. Nylabone® products give your dog something to do for an hour or two every day and during that hour or two, your dog will be taking an active part in keeping his teeth and gums healthy…without even realizing it! That's invaluable to your dog, and valuable to you!

Nylabone® provides fun bones, challenging bones, and *safe* bones. It is an owner's responsibility to recognize safe chew toys from dangerous ones. Your dog will chew and devour anything you give him. Dogs must not be permitted to chew on items that they can break. Pieces of broken objects can do internal damage to a dog, besides ripping the dog's mouth. Cheap plastic or rubber toys can cause stoppage in the intestines; such stoppages are operable only if caught immediately.

The most obvious choices, in this case, may be the worst choice. Natural beef bones were not designed for chewing and cannot take too much pressure from the sides. Due to the abrasive nature of these bones, they should be offered most sparingly. Knuckle bones, though once very popular for dogs, can be easily

Nylabone® is the only plastic dog bone made of 100% virgin nylon, specially processed to create a tough, durable, completely safe bone.

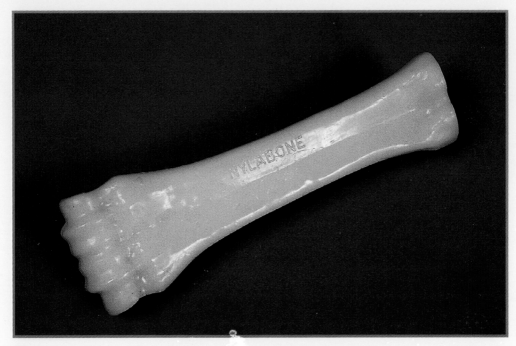

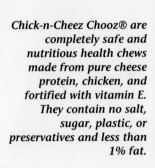

Chick-n-Cheez Chooz® are completely safe and nutritious health chews made from pure cheese protein, chicken, and fortified with vitamin E. They contain no salt, sugar, plastic, or preservatives and less than 1% fat.

chewed up and eaten by dogs. At the very least, digestion is interrupted; at worst, the dog can choke or suffer from intestinal blockage.

When a dog chews hard on a Nylabone®, little bristle-like projections appear on the surface of the bone. These help to clean the dog's teeth and add to the gum-massaging. Given the chemistry of the nylon, the bristle can pass through the dog's intestinal tract without effect. Since nylon is inert, no microorganism can grow on it, and it can be washed in soap and water or sterilized in boiling water or in an autoclave.

For the sake of your dog, his teeth and your own peace of mind, provide your dog with Nylabones®. They have 100 variations from which to choose.

FIGHTING FLEAS

Fleas are very mobile and may be red, black, or brown in color. The adults suck the blood of the host, while the larvae feed on the feces of the adults, which is rich in blood. Flea "dirt" may be seen on the pup as very tiny clusters of blackish specks that look like freshly ground pepper. The eggs of fleas may be laid on the puppy, though they are more commonly laid off the host in a favorable place, such as the bedding. They normally hatch in 4 to 21 days, depending on the temperature, but they can survive for up to 18 months if temperature conditions are not favorable. The larvae are maggot-like and molt a couple of times before forming pupae, which can survive long periods until the temperature, or the vibration of a nearby host, causes them to emerge and jump on a host.

There are a number of effective treatments available, and you should discuss them with your veterinarian, then follow all instructions for the one you choose. Any treatment will involve a product for your puppy or dog and one for the environment, and will require diligence on your part to treat all areas and thoroughly clean your home and yard until the infestation is eradicated.

THE TROUBLE WITH TICKS

Ticks are arthropods of the spider family, which means they have eight legs (though the larvae have six). They bury their headparts into the host and gorge on its blood. They are easily seen as small grain-like creatures sticking out from the skin. They are often picked up when dogs play in fields, but may also arrive in your yard via wild animals—even birds—or stray cats and dogs. Some ticks are species-specific, others are more adaptable and will host on many species.

The cat flea is the most common flea of dogs. It starts feeding soon after it makes contact with the dog.

The deer tick is the most common carrier of Lyme disease. Photo courtesy of Virbac Laboratories, Inc., Fort Worth, Texas.

The most troublesome type of tick is the deer tick, which spreads the deadly Lyme disease that can cripple a dog (or a person). Deer ticks are tiny and very hard to detect. Often, by the time they're big enough to notice, they've been feeding on the dog for a few days—long enough to do their damage. Lyme disease was named for the area of the United States in which it was first detected—Lyme, Connecticut—but has now been diagnosed in almost all parts of the U.S. Your veterinarian can advise you of the danger to your dog(s) in your area, and may suggest your dog be vaccinated for Lyme. Always go over your dog with a fine-toothed flea comb when you come in from walking through any area that may harbor deer ticks, and if your dog is acting unusually sluggish or sore, seek veterinary advice.

Attempts to pull a tick free will invariably leave the headpart in the pup, where it will die and cause an infected wound or abscess. The best way to remove ticks is to dab a strong saline solution, iodine, or alcohol on them. This will numb them, causing them to loosen their hold, at which time they can be removed with forceps. The wound can then be cleaned and covered with an antiseptic ointment. If ticks are common in your area, consult with your vet for a suitable pesticide to be used in kennels, on bedding, and on the puppy or dog.

INSECTS AND OTHER OUTDOOR DANGERS

There are many biting insects, such as mosquitoes, that can cause discomfort to a puppy. Many diseases are transmitted by the males of these species.

A pup can easily get a grass seed or thorn lodged between his pads or in the folds of his ears. These may go unnoticed until an abscess forms.

This is where your daily check of the puppy or dog will do a world of good. If your puppy has been playing in long grass or places where there may be thorns, pine needles, wild animals, or parasites, the check-up is a wise precaution.

SKIN DISORDERS

Apart from problems associated with lesions created by biting pests, a puppy may fall foul to a number of other skin disorders. Examples are ringworm, mange, and eczema. Ringworm is not caused by a worm, but is a fungal infection. It manifests itself as a sore-looking bald circle. If your puppy should have any form of bald patches, let your veterinarian check him over; a microscopic examination can confirm the condition. Many old remedies for ringworm exist, such as iodine, carbolic acid, formalin, and other tinctures, but modern drugs are superior.

Marshy areas are breeding grounds for parasites and insects. Take the proper precautions to protect your AWS from these critters.

Fungal infections can be very difficult to treat, and even more difficult to eradicate, because of the spores. These can withstand most treatments, other than burning, which is the best thing to do with bedding once the condition has been confirmed.

Mange is a general term that can be applied to many skin conditions where the hair falls out and a flaky crust develops and falls away.

Often, dogs will scratch themselves, and this invariably is worse than the original condition, for it opens lesions that are then subject to viral, fungal, or parasitic attack. The cause of the problem can be various species of mites. These either live on skin debris and the hair follicles, which they destroy, or they bury themselves just beneath the skin and feed on the tissue. Applying general remedies from pet stores is not recommended because it is essential to identify the type of mange before a specific treatment is effective.

Eczema is another non-specific term applied to many skin disorders. The condition can be brought about in many ways. Sunburn, chemicals, allergies to foods, drugs, pollens, and even stress can all produce a deterioration of the skin and coat. Given the range of causal factors, treatment can be difficult because the problem is one of identification. It is a case of taking each possibility at a time and trying to correctly diagnose the matter. If the cause is of a dietary nature then you must remove one item at a time in order to find out if the dog is allergic to a given food. It could, of course, be the lack of a nutrient that is the problem, so if the condition persists, you should consult your veterinarian.

INTERNAL DISORDERS

It cannot be overstressed that it is very foolish to attempt to diagnose an internal disorder without the advice of a veterinarian. Take a relatively common problem such as diarrhea. It might be caused by nothing more serious than the puppy hogging a lot of food or eating something that it has never previously eaten. Conversely, it could be the first indication of a potentially fatal disease. It's up to your veterinarian to make the correct diagnosis.

The following symptoms, especially if they accompany each other or are progressively added to earlier symptoms, mean you should visit the veterinarian right away:

Continual vomiting. All dogs vomit from time to time and this is not necessarily a sign of illness. They will eat grass to induce vomiting. It is a natural cleansing process common to many carnivores. However, continued vomiting is a clear sign of a problem. It may be a blockage in the pup's intestinal tract, it may be induced by worms, or it could be due to any number of diseases.

Diarrhea. This, too, may be nothing more than a temporary condition due to many factors. Even a change of home can induce diarrhea, because this often stresses the pup, and invariably there is some change in the diet. If it persists more than 48 hours then something is amiss. If blood is seen in the feces, waste no time at all in taking the dog to the vet.

Running eyes and/or nose. A pup might have a chill and this will cause the eyes and nose to weep. Again, this should quickly clear up if the puppy is placed in a warm environment and away from any drafts. If it does not, and especially if a mucous discharge is seen, then the pup has an illness that must be diagnosed.

Coughing. Prolonged coughing is a sign of a problem, usually of a respiratory nature.

Wheezing. If the pup has difficulty breathing and makes a wheezing sound when breathing, then something is wrong.

Cries when attempting to defecate or urinate. This might only be a minor problem due to the hard state of the feces, but it could be more serious, especially if the pup cries when urinating.

Cries when touched. Obviously, if you do not handle a puppy with care he might yelp. However, if he cries even when lifted gently, then he has an internal problem that becomes apparent when pressure is applied to a given area of the body. Clearly, this must be diagnosed.

Refuses food. Generally, puppies and dogs are greedy creatures when it comes to feeding time. Some might be more fussy, but none should refuse more than one meal. If they go for a number of hours without showing any interest in their food, then something is not as it should be.

General listlessness. All puppies have their off days when they do not seem their usual cheeky, mischievous selves. If this condition persists for more than two days then there is little doubt of a problem. They may not show any of the signs listed, other than perhaps a reduced interest in their food. There are many diseases that can develop internally without displaying obvious clinical signs. Blood, fecal, and other tests are needed in order to identify the disorder before it reaches an advanced state that may not be treatable.

WORMS

There are many species of worms, and a number of these live in the tissues of dogs and most other animals. Many create no problem at all, so you are not even aware they exist. Others can be tolerated in small levels, but become a major problem if they number more than a few. The most common types seen in dogs are roundworms and tapeworms. While roundworms are the greater problem, tapeworms require an intermediate host so are more easily eradicated.

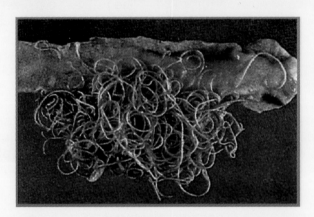

Roundworms are spaghetti-like worms that cause a pot-bellied appearance and dull coat, along with more severe symptoms, such as diarrhea and vomiting. Photo courtesy of Merck AgVet.

Roundworms of the species *Toxocara canis* infest the dog. They may grow to a length of 8 inches (20 cm) and look like strings of spaghetti. The worms feed on the digesting food in the pup's intestines. In chronic cases the puppy will become pot-bellied, have diarrhea, and will vomit. Eventually, he will stop eating, having passed through the stage when he always seems hungry. The worms lay eggs in the puppy and these pass out in his feces. They are then either ingested by the pup, or they are eaten by mice, rats, or beetles. These may then be eaten by the puppy and the life cycle is complete.

Larval worms can migrate to the womb of a pregnant bitch, or to her mammary glands, and this is how they pass to the puppy. The pregnant bitch can be wormed, which will help. The pups can, and should,

Whipworms are hard to find unless you strain your dog's feces, and this is best left to a veterinarian. Pictured here are adult whipworms.

be wormed when they are about two weeks old. Repeat worming every 10 to 14 days and the parasites should be removed. Worms can be extremely dangerous to young puppies, so you should be sure the pup is wormed as a matter of routine.

Tapeworms can be seen as tiny rice-like eggs sticking to the puppy's or dog's anus. They are less destructive, but still undesirable. The eggs are eaten by mice, fleas, rabbits, and other animals that serve as intermediate hosts. They develop into a larval stage and the host must be eaten by the dog in order to complete the chain. Your vet will supply a suitable remedy if tapeworms are seen or suspected. There are other worms, such as hookworms and whipworms, that are also blood suckers. They will make a pup anemic, and blood might be seen in the feces, which can be examined by the vet to confirm their presence. Cleanliness in all matters is the best preventative measure for all worms.

Heartworm infestation in dogs is passed by mosquitoes but can be prevented by a monthly (or daily) treatment that is given orally. Talk to your vet about the risk of heartworm in your area.

BLOAT (GASTRIC DILATATION)

This condition has proved fatal in many dogs, especially large and deep-chested breeds, such as the Weimaraner and the Great Dane. However, any dog can get bloat. It is caused by swallowing air during exercise, food/water gulping or another strenuous task. As many believe, it is not the result of flatulence. The stomach of an affected dog twists, disallowing food and blood flow and resulting in harmful toxins being released into the bloodstream. Death can easily follow if the condition goes undetected.

The best preventative measure is not to feed large meals or exercise your puppy or dog immediately after he has eaten. Veterinarians recommend feeding three smaller meals per day in an elevated feeding rack, adding water to dry food to prevent gulping, and not offering water during mealtimes.

VACCINATIONS

Every puppy, purebred or mixed breed, should be vaccinated against the major canine diseases. These are distemper, leptospirosis, hepatitis, and canine parvovirus. Your puppy may have received a temporary vaccination against distemper before you purchased him, but be sure to ask the breeder to be sure.

The age at which vaccinations are given can vary, but will usually be when the pup is 8 to 12 weeks old. By this time any protection given to the pup by antibodies received from his mother via her initial milk feeds will be losing their strength.

The puppy's immune system works on the basis that the white blood cells engulf and render harmless

Rely on your veterinarian for the most effectual vaccination schedule for your American Water Spaniel puppy.

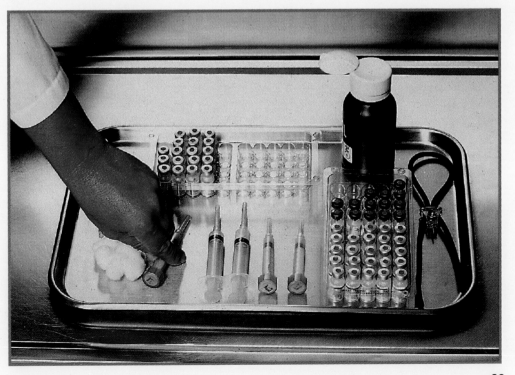

attacking bacteria. However, they must first recognize a potential enemy.

Vaccines are either dead bacteria or they are live, but in very small doses. Either type prompts the pup's defense system to attack them. When a large attack then comes (if it does), the immune system recognizes it and massive numbers of lymphocytes (white blood corpuscles) are mobilized to counter the attack. However, the ability of the cells to recognize these dangerous viruses can diminish over a period of time. It is therefore useful to provide annual reminders about the nature of the enemy. This is done by means of booster injections that keep the immune system on its alert. Immunization is not 100-percent guaranteed to be successful, but is very close. Certainly it is better than giving the puppy no protection.

Dogs are subject to other viral attacks, and if these are of a high-risk factor in your area, then your vet will suggest you have the puppy vaccinated against these as well.

Your puppy or dog should also be vaccinated against the deadly rabies virus. In fact, in many places it is illegal for your dog not to be vaccinated. This is to protect your dog, your family, and the rest of the animal population from this deadly virus that infects the nervous system and causes dementia and death.

ACCIDENTS

All puppies will get their share of bumps and bruises due to the rather energetic way they play. These will usually heal themselves over a few days. Small cuts should be bathed with a suitable disinfectant and then smeared with an antiseptic ointment. If a cut looks more serious, then stem the flow of blood with a towel or makeshift tourniquet and rush the pup to the veterinarian. Never apply so much pressure to the wound that it might restrict the flow of blood to the limb.

In the case of burns you should apply cold water or an ice pack to the surface. If the burn was due to a chemical, then this must be washed away with copious amounts of water. Apply petroleum jelly, or any vegetable oil, to the burn. Trim away the hair if need be. Wrap the dog in a blanket and rush him to the vet. The pup may go into shock, depending on the severity of the burn, and this will result in a lowered blood pressure, which is dangerous and the reason the pup must receive immediate veterinary attention.

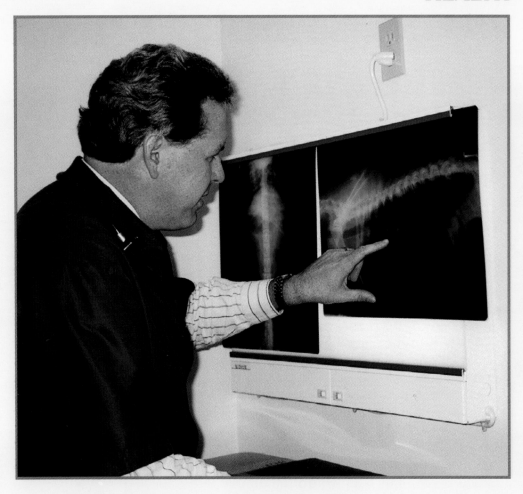

It is a good idea to x-ray the chest and abdomen on any dog hit by a car.

If a broken limb is suspected then try to keep the animal as still as possible. Wrap your pup or dog in a blanket to restrict movement and get him to the veterinarian as soon as possible. Do not move the dog's head so it is tilting backward, as this might result in blood entering the lungs.

Do not let your pup jump up and down from heights, as this can cause considerable shock to the joints. Like all youngsters, puppies do not know when enough is enough, so you must do all their thinking for them.

Provided you apply strict hygiene to all aspects of raising your puppy, and you make daily checks on his physical state, you have done as much as you can to safeguard him during his most vulnerable period. Routine visits to your veterinarian are also recommended, especially while the puppy is under one year of age. The vet may notice something that did not seem important to you.

PET OWNERS & BLOOD PRESSURE

Over the past few years, several scientific studies have documented many health benefits of having pets in our lives. At the State University of New York at Buffalo, for example, Dr. Karen Allen and her colleagues have focused on how physical reactions to psychological stress are influenced by the presence of pets. One such study compared the effect of pets with that of a person's close friend and reported pets to be dramatically better than friends at providing unconditional support. Blood pressure was monitored throughout the study, and, on average, the blood pressure of people under stress who were *with* their pets was 112/75, as compared to 140/95 when they were with the self-selected friends. Heart rate differences were also significantly lower when participants were with their pets. A follow-up study included married couples and looked at the stress-reducing effect of pets versus *spouses*, and found, once again, that pets were dramatically more successful than other people in reducing cardiovascular reactions to stress. An interesting discovery made in this study was that when the spouse and pet were *both* present, heart rate and blood pressure came down dramatically.

Other work by the same researchers has looked at the role of pets in moderating age-related increases in blood pressure. In a study that followed 100 women (half in their 20s and half in their 70s) over six months, it was found that elderly women with few social contacts and *no* pets had blood pressures that were significantly higher (averages of 145/95 compared to 120/80) than elderly women with their beloved pets but few *human* contacts. In other words, elderly women with pets, but no friends, had blood pressures that closely reflected the blood pressures of young women.

This series of studies demonstrates that pets can play an important role in how we handle everyday stress, and shows that biological aging cannot be fully understood without a consideration of the social factors in our lives.

More than best friends or even spouses, pets have a natural calming effect on their humans.

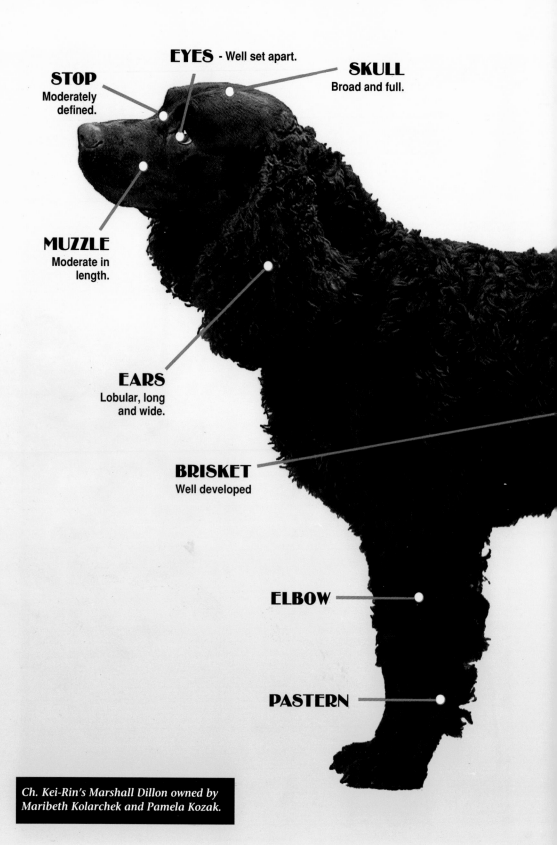

EYES - Well set apart.

SKULL
Broad and full.

STOP
Moderately
defined.

MUZZLE
Moderate in
length.

EARS
Lobular, long
and wide.

BRISKET
Well developed

ELBOW

PASTERN

*Ch. Kei-Rin's Marshall Dillon owned by
Maribeth Kolarchek and Pamela Kozak.*